DAEDALUS HAD A DAUGHTER

DAEDALUS HAD A DAUGHTER

WANDA CAMPBELL

Carolyn Marie Souaid, Editor

Signature EDITIONS

Cover design by Doowah Design.
Photo of Wanda Campbell by Sandy Campbell.

Acknowledgements
Many of these poems have previously appeared in *Haw[Thorn]* (Gaspereau), *The Ways Women Travel* (Willpower), *Harpweaver, New Scriblerus, Queen's Quarterly, Room of One's Own, Vallum* and *Wascana Review*. I am grateful to Anne Simpson, Carolyn Marie Souaid, and Karen Haughian for making this work stronger.

This book was printed on Ancient Forest Friendly paper.
Printed and bound in Canada by Marquis Book Printing Inc.

We acknowledge the support of The Canada Council for the Arts and the Manitoba Arts Council for our publishing program.

Library and Archives Canada Cataloguing in Publication

Campbell, Wanda, 1963–
Daedalus had a daughter / Wanda Campbell.

Poems.
ISBN 978-1-897109-53-3

I. Title.

PS8555.A5439D34 2011 C811'.54 C2011-902256-7

Signature Editions
P.O. Box 206, RPO Corydon, Winnipeg, Manitoba, R3M 3S7
www.signature-editions.com

Together they will scheme and imagine.
Somehow they will find a way
to put their brute heads in the clouds.

Don McKay
"Icarus"

for all women who
find a way

CONTENTS

I.

GROUP OF SEVEN

More than ever was I convinced that the old way of seeing was inadequate to express this big country of ours, her depth, her height, her unbounded wideness, silences too strong to be broken—

Emily Carr
Growing Pains

I. Breakfast in Bed

(oil on canvas, 1897)

> *I think that if you shake the tree, you ought to be*
> *around when the fruit falls to pick it up.*
> *Mary Cassatt*

breakfast is over and cup and saucer gleam
like Saturn's rings at the edge of a solar system
where the child ripens like the sun

in the sage-green night table she keeps who she was

before this child fell into the orbit of her arms
the latch is only an impression of a latch
whether or not it will open depends on what you believe

II. La Vague: The Wave

(onyx and bronze, 1897)

> *They say I leave at night by the window of my tower,*
> *hanging from a red umbrella with which I set fire to the forest!*
> Camille Claudel

dancing women brace themselves
as the wave descends
there is no time to think or kiss

the vagueness of the asylum looms up

causing even bronze to bend
scarlet fabric is futile
against a tsunami of stone

III. Tod und Frau: Death and the Woman

(soft ground etching, 1910)

> *I do not want to die...until I have faithfully made the*
> *most of my talent and cultivated the seed that was*
> *placed in me until the last small twig has grown.*
>
> *Käthe Kollwitz*

the child climbs the woman like a tree
but death in his cape of cross-hatch
has her in a wrestler's hold

to save the saplings she must grow deep

roots spread wide as her crown
when she is felled they will know
her journey by each ring of truth

IV. BLACK CROSS, NEW MEXICO

(oil on canvas, 1929)

> *... big and strong, put together with wooden pegs,*
> *[and behind it those hills that] go on and on — it was like*
> *looking at two miles of gray elephants.*
>
> *Georgia O'Keeffe*

the dark cross is held together
by pegs like dots on drunken dice
or holes in a huge black button

stitched on a pale shirt of sky

she gambles on this great blue garment
never forgetting each day would unravel
but for this selvage of light

V. SCORNED AS TIMBER, BELOVED OF THE SKY

(oil on canvas, 1935)

I was not ready for abstraction. I clung to earth
and her dear shapes, her density, her herbage, her juice.
Emily Carr

for all the trees I have loved and fallen from
(mango and maple, banyan and birch)
my arm in its calligraphied cast I hold out to you

beloved arrow in the curved bow of the earth

outsoaring all calamity and clear-cut
each brush stroke a fletching
that keeps true the flight

VI. Self-Portrait with Monkeys

(oil on canvas, 1943)

I never painted dreams. I painted my own reality.
Frida Kahlo

she has taken flight from a frame
injured beyond imagining
dark wings of her brows like the crows

we drew before details devoured us

she is the bird of paradise
that flies from her ear
as perfect as a peasant prayer

VII. CAGED BIRD

(hand-painted silk, 2006)

> *Silk is a sensual medium. The textures and movement*
> *of the fabric have always inspired my subject matter.*
> *Holly Carr*

like the silkworms that perish
to grant her the supple canvas
of her dreams she is held captive

    by the cramped cocoon of wishing

escapees invite jailbreak
promise an iridescent arc
against the inevitable rain

II.

HAW [THORN]

For my mother
and her birth mother
Mildred Louise Hawthorne
(1913–1967)

HAW

Scarlet

Haw. The fruit of the hawthorn.

when the red stopped   it came back everywhere else
in her nipples ripening like berries
in stretch marks on her belly
in tongues of the town

unwed they said
her father worked for Ruddy Manufacturing
makers of bed springs and bee-keeping supplies
no gear to guard against this sting

he crawled into the big brown bed
of the earth and would not wake
but many people refused to interpret the scarlet A
by its original signification   said it meant Able

when words sharpen like thorns
a crimson lineage blossoms in the blood

PHANTOM LIMB

Haw. Used as a type of a thing of no value. Obs.

she gave up   you
your new parents erected a fence around your origins
old Dr. Livingstone, physician to both your mothers
guarded that dark continent

your father, you say, was a loveable man
but when you cut your long hair the book he gave you
Bobbed Hair, Bossy Wives, and Women Preachers
hinted hellfire

for years your mother hid what she knew
in her underwear drawer then out of the blue hands it to you
your other mother's marriage announcement from the *Toronto Star*
you are 53 and she cut this out when you were ten

maybe with the same scissors you used
to amputate your braids   the pain of what isn't there

1492

Haw. Blue, azure; greyish or greenish-blue. Obs.

Isabel Hawthorne
the gift your mother gave you
that you did not get to keep
what a shame the name

of the queen who sent Columbus
off the edge of the known
you set out to discover if her eyes
are spheres as blue as your own

countless questions nibble
the rigging of your caravel
but scurvy threatens
who knew it would be so far between gardens?

you always bring the wrong thing
when you don't know where you're going

HUSH MONEY

Haw. An utterance marking hesitation,
usually in collocation with hum.

your mother told no tales
but one old lady says she knows your father
was a grandson of the president
of Cockshutt Plough Company

a summer field furrowed
for a February harvest
says his family paid
to keep the whole thing quiet

then hums and haws
will say no more
the one man who could tell
is past telling

trees by the crematorium
murmur a wordless song

EXPO '67

Haw. The nictitating membrane of a horse, etc.

horses have a third eyelid to sweep away dust
without loss of vision
we humans must go blind
or keep looking until our eyes boil

at last you learn she has been dead these thirty years
we were in Canada that year
home from dusty India to see the pavilions of the world
she lay dying but we did not know

lots of strangers were there in Montreal
even my husband-to-be, then five
his address written on his arm — letters against lostness
and me — only three — carrying my one souvenir

a doll in Canadian tartan   not one of those
whose eyes close when you lay her down

Family Tree

Haw: A hedge or fence;
hence, a piece of ground enclosed.

my father's family is as clear as the sap his father
squeezed from the trees each sweet spring
his mother only four at her mother's sick-room door
kids farmed out after the funeral like maple keys in the wind

my mother's mother   a blank
but for the words of her lawyer boss
short, sharp dresser with glasses
addicted to cigarettes

all the rest   gone up in smoke
her body bequeathed for young doctors
to dismantle and discover
where death is born

there is no ground we can go to
there is no ground we can grow from

[THORN]

Paradise Lost

Thorn. A stiff, sharp-pointed projection on the stem of a plant.

the Eden dream is in our blood
flowers of all hue
and without thorn the rose
but we wake on the far side of the sword

in India where I was born
thorns were so vicious
they made fences as good as barbed wire to keep
goats from the garden, sacred cows from the temple

like the thorns
on the forehead of the suffering man
keeping one thief in and one thief out
when darkness fell

in this wild you are a blade between griefs
so brief the gap between roots and withering

CABINET OF CURIOSITIES

Thorn. Anything that causes pain, grief, or trouble.

you say the lump in your breast
felt like a pea under a mattress
they cut it from your flesh but already the crab
had scuttled away, mutations flowing through your body

like stars through the Milky Way
the doctor looked out the window, not at you
they bring on big guns refined in war (surgery, radiation, chemicals)
you bring on small arms perfected in peace (friendship, laughter, prayer)

the princess was *all over black and blue*
from three peas under
twenty mattresses and twenty feather beds
of course she lived happily ever after

the three peas were, however, put into the cabinet of curiosities
where they can still be seen, provided they are not lost

Arsenic and Old Lace

Thorn. In lace-making, pointed projections
used to decorate the cordonnet, etc.

the strip joint I pass on my way
to work advertises exotic dancers
Plenty Up Top, Melanie Melons,
Cindy Staxxx   milkless breasts

are mere decoration, ancient lace
to save them you lose that other decoration
your hair, bobbed since youth
public and private— altogether gone

the witch has shorn your clandestine ladder
Delilah has determined what brings you down
wigs at Sears have names like
Petite Adore and Pure Delight

you choose a cage of
one hundred thousand bars

Geometer Moth

Thorn. Collectors' name for various geometrid moths.

along with advice on how to manage
radiation burns, pain, fatigue, mouth sores, dizziness, bruising,
bleeding, swelling, numbness, kidney damage, hair loss, nausea,
vomiting, diarrhoea, cramps, headaches, heart failure, etcetera

you are given pamphlets
on a positive approach
pretty soon you'll find you are smiling
would you have believed it?

wings stamped with the same fatal design
your bosom buddies die one by one
the goal, says the doctor, is to kill the cancer
without killing you   a fine line

treatment zone tattooed
you return again and again to the flame

Rune

Thorn. The name of the Old English runic letter þ.

how many are there
scored by scalpel, staples, stitches
the ancient alphabet of pain?
one in eight

a disease once distant suddenly everywhere
each year our women dying
one for every kilometre
between Halifax and Calgary

theories sprout like loosestrife
along this dark highway
but no certain knowledge
just a threnody in the throats

of birds on the green gown
that slips from the shoulders of the road

Urchin

Thorn. A spine or spiny process in an animal.

will this be our dark inheritance?
when the spines are gone one sees the exquisite design
on the urchin   even the test that shelters
tenderness cannot protect from gulls

greedy angels dropping urchins
from great heights to shatter on the shore
fragments reveal the mouth a lamp
of fifty tiny bones that scrape sustaining green

named Aristotle's Lantern after the philosopher
who also wrote: *a perfect tragedy should, as we have seen,*
be arranged not on the simple but on the complex plan
we who are daughters   we who have daughters

speech is salvage
it is the mouth that lights our way

III.

GRADUATED TO GLASS

"Well, now that we have seen each other," said the Unicorn,
"if you'll believe in me, I'll believe in you."

Lewis Carroll
Through The Looking-Glass: And What Alice Found There

Snake on Display

I swim sinuous in this aquarium
made dry for me, this new place
        smaller but safer
        no talons, no tires

now I don't have to drag these diamonds
all over kingdom come
        but I keep bumping into the shed bits
        old skins that are and are not me

white and shimmery like silk wedding stockings
crumpled by the bed or cloudy and sad
        like used condoms
        in the grass

the walls of my world are clear
sometimes I look through them
        sometimes I look at them
        and see myself

the sign says DO NOT TAP ON THE GLASS
but they do anyway and my tongue goes in and out
        sniffing
        the intimate air

ACCIDENTAL HONEY

> *The total amount of blood in a pregnant woman's body has increased by approximately 25 percent by the time of delivery.*
>
> Encyclopedia Britannica

my man taps maples over on Arner townline
says maybe a brave hurled his tomahawk at a tree
        flow from the gash thickening
        around red hot stones

accidental honey won from wounding
for centuries this was our sweetness
        cane sugar a luxury from
        a slashed and sunburnt south

this spring I feel the sap that engenders the flower
rising in new veins but loath to labour long to distil
        the blood of trees to treacle
        the buds we bear are few

Naming My Daughters

Natives gave names of animals to boys
summoning sinew, stealth, and speed
        flowers to girls: perfume
        tethered to the silken stalk

even now boys are named for
patriarchs, apostles, ancestors, saints
        while girls' names come from nowhere.
        How to avoid ornamental sobriquet?

Piper is the bird that runs a familiar shore
music of her father's homeland
        heart of a child / gall of a thousand / strength of conviction
        and Alexandra, defender of men and builder of empires

Tilly is the great grandmother with strength
in her sepia eyes and Jay because they won
        their second world series that summer and built
        a nest in the eaves, cells multiplying to swooping blue

Esme is the girl in the Salinger story with the *oddly radiant*
smile wearing a rain-spangled dress of Campbell tartan
        and Bronwen who wrote poems about the *common magic*
        that flares like a match in the ordinary dark

House of Blood

my four-year-old sees blood and offers a Band-Aid
I tell her every month my body builds a house of blood
 that leaks out when no guest comes to call
 taboo is Polynesian for menstruation

the woman driven to the edge of the tribe to sit
alone, dripping danger and magic in a hut of leaves
 in India, the *dhobis* who beat the blood
 from the rags were untouchable

now commercials promise there is nothing we cannot do
(swim, ride, wear white power suits) promise
 we will not be prevented from our life
 as if this has nothing to do with our life

I hold my daughter and dream the day
she too can build a house of blood
 our first and most
 miraculous dwelling

X-RAY

a dislocated elbow yields a glimpse
inside my daughter, shadow shufti of
    humerus, radius, ulna
    petite and prone to slippage

once I could look inside her head
via the diamond window that eased her passage
    but fontanelles no longer pulse
    bone blinds are forever drawn

I know her armour will grow more sophisticated
and opaque, the visor come crashing down
    someday I will see nothing
    but what she wishes me to see

in her lashed green eyes
she may choose like Houdini's wife
    to pass the key in a kiss
    but it will not be to me

TAKING MY DAUGHTERS TUBING

my daughters float down the river
on summer's dark doughnuts
          their long limbs
          shimmering

in the past I would go along to ensure
nobody drowned or drifted away
          but now I'm only expected
          to be there at the other end

when they emerge dripping and breathless
sparkling with river and story
          and so I wait and watch
          summer slide into autumn

apples ripen and scarlet creeper
festoons the old-fashioned poles
          weathered grey crosses
          bearing *parole* and power

sparrows scatter like dark rice against
the gauzy blue veil of sky
          the river rushes past
          the willow; her silver leaves

brush the water like the long hair
of a girl washing her face in a stream
          hoping to catch a glimpse
          as my daughters drift into view

I stand in the middle of
the bridge, suddenly aware
          of how it trembles
          with every crossing

Graduated to Glass

my children have all graduated to glass
gone the plastic in primary colours
        stackable rainbows of sippy cups
        safe from splinter and spill

now they drink, like their parents, from glasses
clear and heavy, holding more and more
        in sizes odd and obscure
        old-fashioned, highball, tumbler

less likely to tip but
sure to shatter if they fall
        dangerous in dishwater
        hazardous underfoot

they use whatever's clean
for whatever's poured
        milk, juice, water, pop,
        but someday beer

and other fuzziness in bottles
that can only be opened by
        corkscrews, jackknives
        or the tough hands of boys

soon it will be goblets of
graduations and weddings
        hardly able to stand
        on so slender a stem

foreign glass stashed in carry-on luggage
cut crystal from Europe, from Mexico
        heavy and hand blown
        brilliantly blue

stemware of anniversaries rimmed with ores
more precious as years and people pass
          and finally beside the bed
          one glass for water for pills

the other for dentures like joke-shop wind-up teeth
the kind that chatter and chatter and chatter
          until they
          stop

Zebra Mussels: An Anniversary Poem

you muscled your way into my blood
in the bilge water of a foreign tanker
    once Niagara's thunder
    thwarted all threats

but now you have picked
the locks of my heart
    it was my own fault
    welcoming the zebras

grace and power defined
in black and white lines
    I couldn't help it
    caught the scent of the exotic

hot breeze off the Serengeti
sunrise over Kilimanjaro
    I should have guessed
    you would thrive in my veins

I listen carefully to scientists
attempting strange solutions
    electric currents and air bubbles
    chemistry on the keel

but it is too late   twenty years later
every contour is encrusted
    the most fragile indigenous
    species have disappeared

but I am learning how to live with you
the Dutch experiment with mussels
        as a living filter by which
        the polluted water of the world

again becomes
sparkling clear
        good enough
        to drink

BARD SALE

Spring cleaning
I gather up the clutter in my head
put it on card tables in the driveway
or blankets on the lawn

you stroll by and say
this would fit Amy
she looks good in green
or ask, does it still work?

I run an extension cord
from the house to prove that it does
sure enough the light goes on
or the music comes through

or the element gets red
we have a four-slice now, I say
so you'll know I'm not getting rid of it
because it's broken or useless

you ask how much
and I make up something on the spot
because I don't really know how much
these things are worth anyway

and couldn't be bothered to put a price
on everything even if I did
you give me coins with names
that rhyme with order, fickle, time

you look at your new old toaster
and see your own face
you are happy
I am happy

IV.

WOMEN AND MEN

what compass would not spin
at these coordinates?

Andrew Steeves
Improbable Cures

Strip Tease

he loves to watch
nature emerge all carving and curve
        grain rising like topography
        under his vehement eyes

a mere glimpse
of breast beneath
        a carelessly buttoned blouse
        is enough for him

all the ancient wiring
firing, sparks leaping
        through the conduits
        of forward flesh

she takes more
more words, more touch
        more time, more tease
        deliberation is her fortress

if it weren't for this difference
they would be so lost in love
        nothing or everything would happen
        all the breathless time

their desire is Braille
embossed in the blood
        it must be touched
        to be understood

Nueés Ardentes

suffer the fire rolling like a cloud
down familiar slopes
        choking
        changing

let go the lava snaking suddenly
from faults in friendship and love
        avalanche of
        fury and flame

eruptions to regret from cracks in every day
passion and anger that end in stone
        or new islands
        in the sea

all is arrogant ash, yet this alone
kept Pompeii safe from vandals and weather
        mortality's
        magic act

a startling record
of the molten moment
        when flight became
        impossible

Everywhere, Hunger After the Garden

I used to argue when Jamie claimed
all my poems had sex in them
    How can this be? I would ask
    Baptist buttons fastened fierce

that was before I had
risen ripe into a lean embrace
    before I had known a man
    in the biblical way

now I know better,
can spot the rollick
    and seethe beneath
    the skin of things

the tide licking up the flats
twice each salty day
    the pull of the planets
    toward the potent sun

bees dragging gold-laden legs
through the heart of every flower
    sky pressing down
    on the thighs of the earth

Wishing the Wild

the singer on TV says we must
make more of the monkey in us
    mate and feed
    go naked under the sun

who knows what sophistication lies
in the language of gesture and grunt
    for the anthill
    you only need one tool

put the stick
in the hole
    draw it out
    swarming

I have found myself wishing the wild
was not driven so far buried so deep
    I have seen hands on the bars
    and recognized them as my own

but when I change channels
I see monkeys from the Amazon
    surviving on fruit so toxic
    they must nightly descend

to the perilous earth
devour dirt to neutralize
    the gorgeous poison
    that keeps them alive

Northing

there should be a system to keep track of people
the way libraries keep track of books
        a magnetic strip down the spine
        that signals withdrawal without consent

so we wouldn't suddenly
come upon a gap in the shelf
        and wonder what belonged there
        what wisdom beyond retrieval and regret

much has vanished from the collection
volumes no one has taken out in years
        the lone narwhal horn elegant as any unicorn's
        in the glass cabinet one could shatter in case of reality

you alone endure   your warm back
a terrain of blessings beneath my fingers
        vertebrae thread like beads on a needle
        steady against the tilting earth

STONING

the sole object that offends you
on this beach littered with male trash
        is this pink plastic carapace of tampon
        empty as a moulted lobster shell

everywhere, bottles, bags, bits of rope
nailed boards, detritus of catch and hunt
        but this alone makes you uneasy
        because it was once inside a body

because it was once slippery with blood
you throw stones until it disappears
        inside that other familiar body
        you can neither fathom nor forget

EDGE

men who don't wear coats
boys who won't wear mittens
    digging in the schoolyard snow
    male hands red and raw

the women I know carry the house with them
right on their backs: parkas, scarves, gloves
    their hair blowing like curtains
    out from under the eaves of their hats

is a man more furred and furnished for squall and fury
determined to deny the border between out and in
    to keep it permeable
    as it has always been for him?

does he walk abroad
in every weather wishing
    the only home he needed
    was his own warm skin?

Ways Women Travel

A story of yours got this one going
so I'm sending it back now, changed of course,
just as each person I love
is a relocation, where I take up
a different place in the world.
Bronwen Wallace

I. Walking

those first stutter steps
toward the ones who got us into
this unpredictable miracle
in the first place

then toddling, skipping, sauntering, striding
until we can walk through and away
hand in hand with someone new
down an aisle strewn with petals and promises

next the long, long corridors of the maternity ward
hands on the small of the back, the curve of the belly
then walking through the wee
with an infant that will not hush

pushing a pram or pulling a wagon
pushing a shopping cart or pulling
a kid past the kaleidoscope
of the corner candy store

eventually we walk for exercise or leisure
admiring the sun on the water
or the way the wind
bends the grass on the dykes

and soon we walk for the cure
as women we know start to die
    we walk to take back the night
    and take back the day

we walk and wonder about women elsewhere
who have no choice but to walk miles and miles
    for water, for work, for what
    we daily take for granted

II. Wheels

rainbow beads on the spokes
of my daughter's tricycle
    slide and twirl, a child's bright rosary
    as she pedals around her little world

I myself ride on four wheels
speed spilling from me like water
    from iridescent feathers
    and I steer the fifth

hands at ten and two as if it were
a clock I could control
    going farther and faster
    on buses and trains

and occasionally planes
landing gear descending like
    the webbed feet of geese
    on a yet unfrozen pond

but later I see an
old woman on a tricycle
    decorated not with
    tassels and beads

but an orange triangle like
those on Mennonite carriages
    and large machinery indicating
    slow-moving, indicating caution

and the circle
comes round
    no hair, no teeth
    no memory

I, of the more-wheeled-in-between,
am reminded how brief this arc
    and resolve to be gracious
    to those less swift and sure

III. Wings

for Jessica Whitney Dubroff (1989-1996)

Women Fly. That's the claim
embroidered in black letters
 on her pink baseball cap
 forever seven, she graces

the cover of ***TIME***
no longer a little girl
 failing to pilot a plane
 across the continent but a parable

I read on my flight to Toronto
while outside my window
 the earth turns under her green quilt
 like a pregnant woman seeking ease

I'm going to fly till I die says Jessica
straight down like a lawn dart says an eyewitness
 we know, in the end, the grown-up pilot had taken over
 because his arms were more fractured than hers

Women Fly

Harriet Quimby, first woman to fly the English Channel
but everyone too busy salvaging Titanic dead to notice
 months later she was flung from her plane
 to be swallowed by that same ocean

Amelia Earhart in leather and pearls, swallowed
by the other ocean, then Christa McAuliffe
 first civilian in space
 swallowed by the sky

there were women who broke records
without being broken themselves but they
          are not the ones we remember
          Daedalus had a daughter

IV. WONDER

she is startled by tulips
igniting like flame in a porcelain vase
        she bends down to look at bugs and small
        flowers her daughter calls *chimpansies*

she walks the beach in search
of pebbles as round as the world
        or driftwood in clever and curious shapes
        roots that have grown around rocks

everywhere she sees the light hand of God
and the devil's dark footprint
        dawn and dusk are the fringes
        of the rag rug she walks upon

as she tucks her into bed
she is struck by the small perfect shape
        of her daughter's ear, like a shell
        in which she can hear tomorrow

she moves in wonder even when she is standing still
it is what shakes her awake in the middle of the night
        or calls to her from the
        portraits she loves

it is what echoes over and through
the mind's menace, the body's betrayal
        and speaks in words of women
        she has grown to trust

these visions, these voices
waves of wonder
        that lift us
        to the other shore

SUSANNA

> *"Never fret about the china," said Moodie; "thank God, the man and the horses are uninjured." I should have felt more thankful had the crocks been spared too.*
>
> *Susanna Moodie (1803-1885)*

back in the old country, Sand
falls through men's clothing
    one grain at a time, but no trousers
    can disguise the hourglass

wading through drifts
of dandelions and desire, you learn
    the wave that heaves us on
    will never bear us back

wait for him in winter
leaning on the shanty door
    compose a sleigh bell song
    shored against the howling

mourn the china
shattered in the snow
    the pattern displays a daughter
    following her beloved

to the far side of the sea
willows weep but we
    fly up from fragments
    as newly minted doves

WOOLF

Virginia Woolf is the Jackie Robinson
of women's writing.
Will, a student

the one man in a class full of women
surprised to be for once a minority
wearing short sleeves even in winter
bears gifts in his hard brown arms

knowing they both insisted we are as good as you
knowing they both wanted fans to look past the colour
of their difference to the music of their swing
such jazz and grace and skill at stealing

they entered their own rooms
but found them bleak and bare
the great experiment
took its toll

she, 59, loading her pockets
with stones the size of baseballs
and walking into the stream
of the unconscious

he, 53, leaning on a cane instead of a bat, almost blind
saying I never had it made, but Jesse Jackson at his funeral
calling him a rock in the water
ripples and waves

Ever After

> *"But if you take my voice from me," said the princess,*
> *"What have I left with which to charm the prince?"*
> *"Thy graceful form," replied the witch:*
> *"thy modest gait, and speaking eyes."*
>
> *Hans Christian Andersen*
> The Little Mermaid

when my sister was in medical school
they called their cadaver Lady Di
  now she really is dead
  the fairy tale over

the little mermaid was told
You will retain your graceful movements
  and no dancer will move so lightly
  but every step you take will

cause you pain all but unbearable —
it will seem to you as if you were walking
  on the sharp edges of swords
  — and your blood will flow.

she replied, *Still I will venture*
I admit to rising at dawn
  to watch her sail into history
  with her cargo of lilies

she has turned to foam on the sea
of flowers that lap against
  the closed gates
  of the palace

NO PYGMALION

To resurrect
now
would take a miracle.
Hilary Thompson (1943–2009)
"Skinny Dipping at Easter"

betrayed and upheld
by silver crutches
she tells the truth
we want to be immortal

would suffer the swings of hammer and chisel
bear the palette knife against our skin
to become
a work of art

we sidle up to poets and painters
anyone with the power
to sculpt us so exquisitely
time will be out of luck

Pygmalion prayed his gal would turn
to flesh but we dream in marble
how I hoped in the high school gymnasium
Alden Nowlan might make of me a poem

but what had I done to earn eternity?
this is the chiaroscuro lesson that finally comes
the only pigments we can
persuade will be our own

NOT ONLY

for Anne

> *As often as he crossed the pane, I could fancy*
> *that a thread of vital light became visible.*
>
> *Virginia Woolf*
> *"The Death of a Moth"*

of course it would be the creature that came
when she closed her eyes in the holy dark
Woolf's tiny fluttering moth, like her mark
on the wall, hard to decipher and name

a nail, a rose-leaf, a crack in the wood?
antennae like fronds of exotic ferns
are how she listens and how she learns
how the compass of shine is understood

a poet alone but never lonely
in that still place where light and dark collide
wrestles with her angel, her spirit guide
this is what she fights for—not only

to desire the vision but to see it
not just be drawn to the flame but be it

WATER NYMPH

purple pickerel, water lilies white
and yellow, wreath the liquid darkness of
her hair that sparkles with the sun's first light
and reflects a blue heron flying above

but for a snarl of reeds or braid of stone
my canoe slides through, a tortoiseshell comb
untangling her tresses and making them shine
with a silky wake of ripples and foam

greybeards lean in to counsel modesty
but nothing can dispel her youthful grace
elders call her vain and shallow but she
has turned her exquisitely unlined face

to a far deeper world I cannot see
though liminal wisdom whispers still to me

Swimming

Let's call it swimming.
Martha and the Muffins

afternoons in water were bright and long
that summer the boys began to be men
we found the sparkle of minnow and song
practised diving deep again and again

we could no longer see our wavering limbs
sunlight scattering the surface like sword-sparks
against a shield   usually the one who swims
leaves no trail but your careful pencil marks

return us to green seasons by the shore
transparent quench spilling from our sunburned
shoulders loud laughter splash and squint   what more
could I ask for?   and now because I've learned

enough of anything becomes opaque
I won't take for granted this cool clear lake

Else

What he did talk about was pain and darkness
and how when the world loses its light it can get easier
and easier to forget what the light is like.
Ryan Dodington

he came to tell me why he didn't get
his story done   he said he missed the dead
line writing to the newspaper instead
in his voice no excuse and no regret

Football players beat the shit out of two
guys who live in my house. Time has shown
police do nothing. We must mind our own.
I had to speak up. What else could I do?

I looked at him   he looked back at me
some moments force a clearing of debris

I did not question   I did not insist
because this was a case as we both knew
of words doing what they're supposed to do
become the jaw that intercepts the fist

Nights at the Irving Station

No one told me
to beware your bracelets,
the winds I could expect
from your small breasts.
Irving Layton, "Song for a Late Hour"

at this late
hour all the stations
are closed except the Irving
out by the highway which pumps
gas all night long and you are driving
home from a documentary on the life of Layton

and can't help
wondering how
many sturdy sedans
and sleek little sports coupes
he stuck his high octane nozzle into
black bras stretched tight across their bumpers

Faye was the
first he married
(for pity he said, and not
for love) then Betty who fled
to California where nights were not as long
Aviva the Australian was the most enduring muse

then Harriet
gave him grief and a
Gucci bag   before Anna became
the fifth and last wife of Flamplatz many
more became poems including Priscilla, Margaret
Francesca, Sandra and the girl with wide-apart eyes

by then his
desire had burned
a colossal hole in the red carpet
of ozone that keeps out the killer sun
he surprised everyone by asking that his ashes
be scattered around the base of an anonymous tree

fossil fuel of the future

Epicure

Nothing is enough for the man to whom enough is too little.
Epicurus

they
call it affair
but it should be
unfair because it means you
have walked away from the one

who gave
you a chance
when you were little
more than raw ingredients
unmeasured / unmixed / undone

the one
who divined that
you would one day be
delicious and was prepared
to take you on, to season to taste

to stand
by you during
blades and beaters
whipping and whisking
the heartache and the heat

now you are
as rare and risen
as a successful soufflé
you have the balls to back out
on the one who saw you through

who refused to let you burn

Why a Woman is Like a Kik-Step

I had the story, bit by bit, from various people,
and, as generally happens in such cases,
each time it was a different story.
Edith Wharton
Ethan Frome

she looks
like a dark shamrock that
Saint Patrick says stands for faith
hope and love blooming in the library aisle
or a burned version of the clover rolls she made
with her grandmother rolling the dough into three
little balls that expanded as beautifully as the universe

she's built
like a 3D ladder
humble enough to bear
the boot and be only two rungs tall
or like a small circus elephant's stool
with a 10-year warranty and a 500 lb download

she works
like a dignified
double-decker skateboard
with wheels that lock for security
or like walkers that were banned because babies
were rolling blissfully down staircases and over cliffs

she's named
like a military march
a fox trot in 4/4 time and a hip
hop move you can see for yourself on
YouTube or like the title of a bill bissett poem
that leaves out all letters that don't earn their keep

she endures
like the St. Lawrence Seaway
still flowing slick as silver, as ahead of
her time as the Avro Arrow also from1957, a 50th
anniversary edition has quotes from Salinger, Hemingway
Wharton, Cervantes, Twain, Dickens and Defoe right in the tread

that takes you up to all the words you want to reach

STRAP

The discrimination represented by section 43 produces the most drastic effect in sending the message that children, as a group, are less worthy of protection of their bodies than anyone else.

Supreme Court Ruling against
School Corporal Punishment, 2004

as a boy
he learned the
strap was a leather
ghoul that haunted him
and punished his flesh still
echoing the razor it sharpened
and the flayed hide which gave it birth

as a girl
she learned the
strap was a lacy
ghost that haunted him
and punished his flesh still
echoing bare shoulders and breasts
upheld by architecture of satin and hooks

his father
used his own belt or
when he was feeling lazy
the dog leash and the teacher
used the strap that hung by the board
dark as an exclamation mark or feeling kind
the ruler that measured each inch he was given.

her mother
used her own bra or
when she was feeling lazy
the merry widow and the girl
next door undressing in the window
used her baby doll p.js or feeling kind
nothing more than her shadowed curves

early on
both learned
you could take a
strap and load it like
a gun that you hold to the
head of those weaker than you

to make them dance

Sister Twister

> *Treat all such events seriously and take appropriate safety precautions if they are occurring or expected in your area.*
> *Environment Canada Website*

brothers
get physical
the list of things
my beloved's brother did
to him goes on and on   punching
throwing hot chilies in his eager eyes
disconnecting the brake lines on his bicycle

sisters
are more subtle
using secrets to ambush
hijacking moments that matter most
yelling *fuck off* outside the Baptist church
sticks and stones your mother said but you both
know it's more fun to be the tornado than the path

twister sisters
is the name they give
this category of weather
like tornadoes but not as dangerous
wall clouds, waterspouts, funnel clouds
gustnadoes, plough winds, dust devils   people don't die
but whatever's not bolted down gets torn up or tossed around

like the game
that ties you up in knots
you try to follow directions without
falling into primary puddles plus green
(green light, green with envy, little green apples)
but inevitably someone touches down and is eliminated
you refuse to be a storm chaser driving wildly into the eye

instead you seek
to build a structure sturdy
enough to withstand the numbers
12 steps, 10 commandments, 9 months, 7 vices
and now the 6 levels of the Fujita Scale (light, moderate
considerable, severe, devastating, incredible, inconceivable)
tether the lightness and do all you can to stay unbroken hoping

survival is the serious side of love

Erratics Maud and Michael

I want to be done with metaphors. I want to see the thing itself.
Michael Ignatieff, Scar Tissue

it takes
you a minute
to know the man out of place
nearly a thousand miles from Stornoway
surprising here in this art gallery by the sea
a boulder different from local bedrock   glacial erratic

you are
both looking at the house
of Maud dragged far from where
she used to be   bluebirds dazzle the door
scarlet flowers burn up the stove and tiny staircase
daisies on the dustpan, tulips triumphant against the glass

while back
in Marshalltown
on Nova Scotia's other coast
a tiny shadow house in Cherubini
steel marks where the real once stood
as a childlike chalice for vivid and defiant joy

you greet
the man who would be
king of your country, knowing her
whole house could fit in the entrance hall of his
with its Victorian table and regency chairs, portrait of
an exiled princess   marble sculpture named *New Born Pride*

in the
gallery lobby
hangs a giant model of a plane
a wooden skeleton that casts captivating shadows
you don't learn until later that it's a Superfortress, the one
that dropped the bomb, burning flowers and stripes into the skin

shadows more artful than the thing itself

WAVES

for Ursula

Every act of pity
is a form of prayer.
Susan Musgrave

hospital
and hospitality
share the same rich root
I know that I have talked too much
and said too little   I have spilled my sorrow like milk
over her kitchen table with the place mats striped with brightness
the tiny loaves of bread and the homemade jam in the cut glass bowl

she advises
removing the eggs
one intends to cook for breakfast
before rolling one's kayak   she believes
merely decorative trees should be replaced
with ones that feed people, fruit being messy
but essential in these uncertain and famished times

she teaches
me what to do with
gifts I do not understand
the green porcelain cow of confusion
is photographed tanning in the meadow or walking the beach
the fruit loaf of forgetting so hardened by neglect becomes the
stollen of solicitude carried forth on one's journey as an honoured guest

she advocates
attentiveness   when I
wake with birdsong and dawn
the flowering tree I did not notice in the dark
is alive with pastel eggs that sparkle and spin   growing old
she says is like the erosion of mountains, a transformation from
formidable to fertile, a slow glaciation smoothing our fears and failures

language can be
trained to ebb and flow
like waves   she knows how
to choose good words and she has chosen mine
taking pity restoring hope   she says listeners are enchanted
she gives me good words to pack in my suitcase and carry home
in the topography of prayer and poetry, the steeper the way,
the closer the lines

soon I will be flying over mountains

NOT DEPARTED

Oh the sisters of mercy, they are not departed or gone.
They were waiting for me when I thought that I just can't go on.
Leonard Cohen

driving the Eastern
shore Marine Drive stops
suddenly at the edge of the river
and we have no choice but to wait
for the ferryman from the far side to fetch us
the cable turning taut in the black water as he comes near

we see three
porcupines, not as
roadkill on the route where grass
rises through the asphalt like stubble
on an ancient face, but still wandering the green
like kings, their backs bearing the quillwork of the future

back in Canso
Don McLean sings of the day
the music died and we hear how
when Flight 797 caught fire Stan went back
to save the others, his deep voice leading them through the flames
the way "Rise Again" pulled a shipwrecked man through a night of waves

meanwhile in Iran
a journalist is being tortured
though he has done nothing wrong
beaten in his grave of a cell he will want to break
lenses that help him see and use the shards to slit his wrists
Never look up, his tormentors tell him, but in a dream he does

two women
who remind him of his sister
stolen by leukemia soothe his suffering
suddenly all songs become secrets to survival
women and men who call through fog and flame
voices of hope hovering over the flood like a dove

they are sisters of mercy   brothers of love

Notes

Title: Daedalus ("cunning worker") created both the Cretan labyrinth and the wings that allowed him and his son Icarus to escape. The title phrase is taken from "Wings," part three of "Ways Women Travel," a poem about women in aviation.

Group of Seven: Each of these seven ekphrastic poems is titled after the work of art that inspired it created by the artist quoted in the epigraph. The works are readily accessible on the World Wide Web.

Haw [Thorn]: Hawthorne was the surname of my mother's birth mother. The twelve poems respond to six definitions of "haw" and six definitions of "thorn" as found in the *Oxford English Dictionary*.

Scarlet: Nathanial Hawthorne's *Scarlet Letter* (1850).

Phantom Limb: *Bobbed Hair, Bossy Wives, and Women Preachers* (1941) by John R. Rice.

Paradise Lost: John Milton's *Paradise Lost* (1667) Book 4, line 256.

Cabinet of Curiosities: "The Real Princess" (1835) by Hans Christian Andersen, more popularly known as "The Princess and the Pea."

Urchin: Aristotle's *Poetics* (c.335 BC) Chapter 13.

Naming My Daughters: Quotations are from Margaret Laurence's description of Piper Gunn in *The Diviners* (1974), J.D. Salinger's "For Esme—With Love and Squalor" from *Nine Stories* (1953) and Bronwen Wallace's *Common Magic* (1985).

Not Only: The second quotation is from Woolf's story "The Mark on the Wall."

Ways Women Travel: Epigraph from Bronwen Wallace's poem "Bones" from *The Stubborn Particulars of Grace* (1987).

iii. Wings: Jessica Whitney Dubroff (1989–1996) attempted to be the youngest person to fly across America. Her story is told in a *TIME* magazine article dated April 22, 1996.

Ever After: This poem commemorates the death of Diana, Princess of Wales (1961–1997).

Nights at the Irving Station: Born Israel Lazarovitch, Canadian poet Irving Layton (1912–2006) was given the nickname *Flamplatz* (Yiddish for "exploding flame") by his mother.

Erratics Maud and Michael: The painted house of folk artist Maud Lewis (1903–1970)was relocated from its original location near Digby to the Art Gallery of Nova Scotia in Halifax. The wooden plane is the work of artist Niall Donaghy.

Not Departed: Canadian folk musician Stan Rogers (1949–1983) died in a fire aboard Air Canada Flight 797 at the Cincinnati Airport. The headliner at the 2009 Stan Rogers Folk Festival (Canso, Nova Scotia) was Don McLean, whose song "American Pie" concerns the 1959 plane crash that killed musicians Buddy Holly, Ritchie Valens, and the Big Bopper. Stan Rogers' song "The Mary Ellen Carter," often referred to as "Rise Again" because of the chorus lyrics, is credited by Robert Cusick with helping him to survive the wreck of the *Marine Electric* on February 12, 1983. Iranian Canadian journalist Maziar Bahari was imprisoned and tortured by the Iranian government between June 21 and October 17, 2009. Bahari credits the songs of Leonard Cohen with creating a "parallel universe" that allowed him to endure.

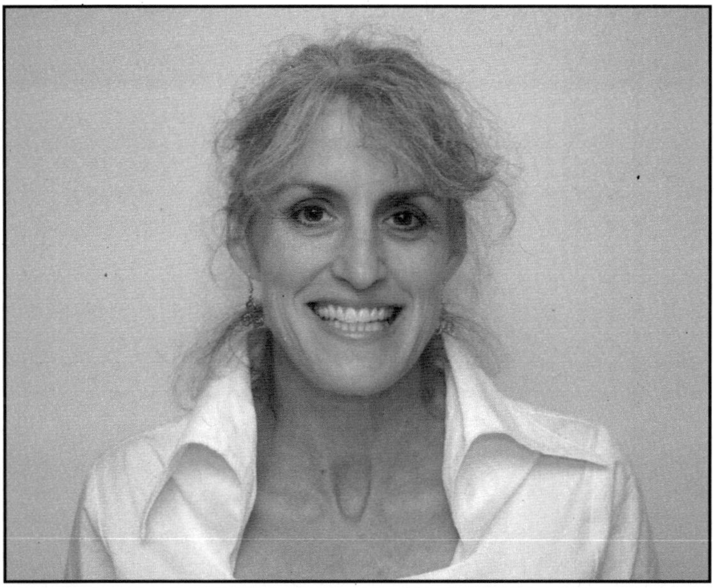

ABOUT THE AUTHOR

Wanda Campbell was born in South India and came to Canada at the age of ten. With her husband and three daughters she has camped in National Parks in every province in Canada and has lived and worked in New Brunswick and Ontario. She now lives in Wolfville, Nova Scotia, where she teaches Creative Writing at Acadia University in view of the highest tides in the world.

She has published three collections of poetry: *Sky Fishing* (Black Moss), *Looking for Lucy* (Leaf) and *Grace* (Blue Grama). She has also edited literature anthologies for Penguin and an anthology of early Canadian women poets called *Hidden Rooms*. Her creative work has appeared in journals from coast to coast including *Antigonish Review, Dalhousie Review, Descant, existere, Fiddlehead, Gaspereau Review, Grain, Harpweaver, New Quarterly, Queen's Quarterly, Room of One's Own, Vallum, Wascana Review, Windsor Review* and in the anthologies *Body Language* and *Landmarks*.

Eco-Audit
Printing this book using Rolland Enviro 100 Book instead of virgin fibres paper saved the following resources:

Trees	Solid Waste	Water	Air Emissions
1	71 kg	4,698 L	185 kg